PROMOTING
PARTN

IDEAS FOR AN AC

CW00405119

Prepared by
Graham Atherton,
Senior Research Officer.

.

Scottish Consumer Council
314 St Vincent Street
Glasgow
G3 8XW

Scottish Consumer Council
314 St. Vincent Street
Glasgow G3 8XW

© Crown copyright 1991
  First published 1991

Illustrations by 'Larry'

ISBN 0 11 494155 6

Contents

Page

Preface   5

Acknowledgements   7

1   Introduction   9

2   **Why parents matter**   12
     parents as educators - parents and schooling -
     parental influences - the changing role of
     parents in schooling - parents as
     partners with staff.

3   **Bringing home and school together**   17
     creating a parent-friendly school -
     parent-teacher consultations - private
     consultations - group consultations -
     other considerations - home-school
     contact: other approaches.

4   **Keeping parents informed**   33
     types of written information for
     parents - content of reports - preparation of
     reports - the school handbook -
     presentation and production.

5   **Representing parents**   41
     Scope - role of school board members -
     dealing with representations -
     school boards and PA/PTAs -
     school boards and parents' groups -
     federations/confederation of school boards.

6   **School boards and home-school**   48
     contact: the way forward.

Appendix 1: school boards and the law   50

Appendix 2: recommended reading   76

Appendix 3: useful addresses   81

Preface

With the setting up of school boards in Scotland, along with other changes in educational legislation, recognition is being given to the crucial role parents have to play in their children's schooling. School boards have special duties to promote home-school links, encourage the formation of parents' and parent-teacher associations, consider parents' views on various matters, and represent parents' viewpoints in dealings with the headteacher and the education authority. In the SCC's view, school boards thus constitute a major new landmark in bringing parents and schools closer together.

This guide suggests how school boards might approach this task. Although school boards have various other functions as well, such as approving spending on school books and materials and promoting community use of the school, we believe their role in linking home and school is their most important one.

We start from the principle that parents as well as teachers are their child's educators and that home and school need to work together in a spirit of equal partnership. Research shows that a child's progress at school is often profoundly influenced by support and encouragement from home. This means that parents should be given ample opportunity and encouragement to meet school staff, keep themselves well informed about their children's schooling, and make their concerns and points of view known.

Although by no means the first or, it is to be hoped, the last word on home-school liaison, this booklet is the first of its kind to offer practical ideas on this topic for school boards for possible action at school level. The ideas are presented here as *suggestions* and not as *prescriptions,* and this publication will have been fully successful if it encourages school boards to develop their own ideas and initiatives for promoting home-school links. The SCC would be very interested in hearing from school boards initiating work or developments in this area.

This booklet, we believe, will not only appeal to school board members but also to parents' and parent-teacher associations, school board support staff, individual teachers and parents and all with an interest in promoting effective home-school partnership. As a parent member of a school board myself, I hope that you will find this booklet useful.

Deirdre Hutton
Chairman

Acknowledgements

The SCC would like to thank the following individuals and organisations for their comments on drafts of the text:

Andrew Dickson, School Boards Support Unit, Scottish Office Education Department.

John Hart, Parent and Teacher.

John Harvard, Scottish Centre for Studies in School Administration.

David Semple, Association of Directors of Education in Scotland.

Harry Smith, Scottish Parent Teacher Council.

Bill Thomson, Jordanhill College of Education.

We are also grateful to officials, including school board support staff, from the following education authorities who offered comments:

Borders Regional Council

Central Regional Council

Highland Regional Council

Lothian Regional Council

Strathclyde Regional Council

Tayside Regional Council

Finally, we would like to offer our special thanks to Alastair Macbeth, Education Department, Glasgow University, author of several publications on home-school matters, who provided detailed comments and guidance throughout the preparation of the text.

Edited by: Katie Carr

Typescript: Muriel Adam.

1. Introduction

School boards offer parents important opportunities to become involved in children's schooling. One of the main functions of the boards, under section 12 of the School Boards (Scotland) Act 1988, is to promote contact between parents and school, including the formation of parents' or parent-teacher associations (PA/PTAs) where these do not already exist. In this respect, school boards have a particularly important part to play in promoting the role of parents as educational partners with teachers in children's schooling. This role is reflected in the law which makes parents primarily responsible for their children's education. The view that parents should have such a role is also backed by research, which shows that support and encouragement from the home is strongly related to achievement at school.

School boards can play a particularly useful role in creating opportunities for parents and teachers to meet one another, for home and school to communicate effectively with one another, and for the schooling system in general to be responsive to parent-teacher concerns. They also function as an important mechanism through which schools may render accounts of their activities, for example, in the curriculum (what is taught), in the assessment of pupils, in teaching methods, in school discipline, and so on. The boards have a duty to take account of the views of parents on matters they are dealing with and to report back to parents if called on to do so. These and other functions of the board are explained in more detail in *Appendix 1: school boards and the law.*

The law gives school boards only limited powers to *control* what takes place in school. School boards cannot, for example, decide what should be taught at school or how the school should be staffed. They do, however, have considerable scope for influencing school policies or practices and, within the limits of the law and the availability of resources (money, staff), they can *initiate* various activities of their own. School boards can, for example, make their views known on any aspect of school policy or practice, including curriculum or assessment matters, and they are entitled to have their views considered and replied to by the headteacher or the education authority. They are expected to observe due confidentiality when discussing staffing matters. They can also ask to take responsibility for various activities delegated to them. They could, for example, be given responsibility for the production of the school's handbook for parents. School boards cannot, however, be given control over the curriculum, assessment of pupils, hiring and firing of staff and certain other matters laid down by law - see Appendix 1 for further details. Under the Self Governing Schools (Scotland) Act 1989, the school board can nevertheless take over the complete running of the school if a majority of parents wish and the Secretary of State agrees.

School boards, then, may be seen not simply as passive bodies endorsing or fitting in with initiatives from the headteacher or the education authority, but as active bodies of teachers and parents working together to generate ideas and initiatives of their own. In his book *School Boards: from purpose to practice*, Alastair Macbeth underlines the importance of school boards having their own clearly defined purposes and goals from the start if they are to develop a good sense of achievement. Of particular interest and relevance to school boards in promoting home-school links are the following kinds of purpose or objectives:

*   promoting the educational well-being and development of children, for example, by encouraging support from the home and making parents aware of their educational responsibilities;

*   supporting the work of staff, for example, by spreading understanding among parents about what is taught and approaches to learning and teaching;

*   assisting with the efficient running of the school, for example, by providing parents with advice and information about opportunities and arrangements for visiting the school and meeting staff;

*   involving parents in key decision-making or policy-making processes, for example, through consultations with parents' groups at the school or through representation of parental concerns at education authority level or beyond;

*   monitoring the school's performance, for example, in reporting and commenting on the school's policies, practices, achievements and difficulties.

School boards need to be clear at the outset what purposes they wish to fulfil and why. In meeting their legal duty to promote home-school links, school boards would be expected to pursue the above kinds of objective.

In preparing this booklet, we have been made only too well-aware of the difficulties which may confront school boards in achieving various objectives. What school boards can achieve will obviously be affected by:

*   the existing powers and functions of the school board, including any delegated functions;

10

*   the commitment, motivation and experience of school board members themselves and the trust and respect they command among the parents and staff they represent;

*   the school's current record of achievement in promoting good home-school links - school boards at schools with a well-developed system of home-school liaison will clearly be in a different position from those at schools with a less-developed one;

*   the availability of staff time - in particular, teachers' conditions of service, which currently limit non-voluntary contact time with parents to up to 30 hours a year;

*   the budget of the school board for meeting administrative, training and other running costs;

*   the readiness of school staff and parents to work together as educational partners, talking with mutual respect and in an open, democratic spirit even on contentious issues in furtherance of the educational welfare of children.

School boards will need to make their own assessments of the scope for developing home-school liaison at their school in the light of the above sorts of consideration. Many of the ideas presented in this booklet are derived from good professional practice and may be implemented at little or no extra cost. Depending on school circumstances, however, some others may require additional money or staffing - for example, home visiting schemes - and school boards will need to consider very carefully whether to press for extra resources, at education authority or central government level, in order to pursue such initiatives.

2. Why parents matter

Parents as educators

Parents are the educators of their children from the moment of birth. They stimulate their child's learning and development through play and other home-based activities. They help to foster their children's language and communication skills through listening and talking to their children. And they give their children opportunities to explore the world around them through books, recreation, new experiences and so on. Parents also influence their children's development through their own example, attitudes, beliefs, behaviour, pursuits, and so forth. The educational role of parents is recognised in law. Under section 30 of the Education (Scotland)) Act, parents are under a legal duty to ensure that their children receive "efficient education" once they are of school age (ages 5-16 years approximately). They normally do this by making sure that their children attend school regularly. Under Section 28 of the Act, the education authority must also take into account the general principle that children are to be educated in accordance with the wishes of their parents.

Parents and schooling

Less than 15 per cent of a child's waking life from birth to 16 is spent in school. A child continues to learn while at home - for example, through leisure reading and the pursuit of hobbies and pastimes. This means that children bring into school knowledge and skills acquired in the home; for example some children learn to read or use computers well before they start school. In these ways, the home can have a decisive influence on progress at school. This is particularly important in the child's early years of schooling, but the home is likely to have a role to play throughout schooling and later education. A key challenge to school boards, and to the educational system as a whole, is to help harness this home learning, and the support that parents can give, to help children to take advantage of the range of educational opportunities that formal schooling can offer.

Parental influences

Parents influence their children's educational development in a number of important ways:

* Through their own *attitudes* to education, which, as research has indicated, may carry as much if not more weight than the schooling process itself or other factors, such as inheritance, parental income or

social class. Parents with positive attitudes to education are likely to bring up children well motivated to learn.

*   Through their own *understanding* of the schooling system. Parents who are well informed about their child's schooling are likely to be in a good position to give their children support and encouragement. This is not just a matter of parents themselves making the effort to become properly informed, but it also means the school system itself giving parents every opportunity and encouragement to do so.

*   Through their own *contact* with their children's teachers. Parents who are in regular contact with teachers are likely to be well placed to judge how well their children are doing at school and in a good position to work out what role they as parents can play at home.

*   Through the day-to-day *support* they give to their children, by helping them to cope with any emotional, practical and other problems associated with their schooling.

Through their legal duty to promote home-school links, school boards have an important part to play in helping to ensure that these parental influences are brought to bear in a positive way.

The changing role of parents in schooling

In times past, parents were not, on the whole, encouraged to become involved in children's schooling beyond making sure that their children attended school regularly and, perhaps, making the occasional visit to the school to hear reports on their child's progress or take part in fund-raising, social or other functions. They were not expected to take an active interest in what or how children were taught. Over the last two decades or so, however, more and more schools have opened their doors to parents for discussion and consultation on a wider range of issues, although some schools have moved much further than others in this direction. Parents are being seen as major stakeholders in the schooling system and not simply as passive spectators. This change has been prompted by the following considerations:

*   As indicated already, a great deal of learning already takes place outwith school, with parents having considerable influence on their child's development, including achievement at school. If parents are to provide appropriate support at home, it is likely that they will have to become involved in central aspects of their children's schooling. Such support means strengthening the relationships

between parents and teachers and breaking down any barriers to parent-teacher communication.

* In addition to this, parents may be viewed as in some respects the "clients" of educational services, through which the service providers are bound by law and good professional practice to consult parents regularly about their children's schooling. Under section 30 of the 1980 Act, parents need not send their child to a school run by the education authority if they can show that they have made suitable alternative arrangements of their own, at home or at a private school. Parents in effect are "contracting out" the provision of education for their child when they arrange to send their child to an education authority school in the ordinary way. Further support for this view of parents as clients of educational services comes from section 28 of the Act which, as already mentioned above, requires the education authority to take into consideration the general principle that children should be educated in accordance with the wishes of their parents. Finally, teachers are bound by their own conditions of service to spend up to 30 hours "contact time" a year with parents.

* Local authorities, as the main providers of educational services, are democratically and financially accountable to parents as electors and community charge payers voting and paying for those services. This means that they must explain and justify their policies and practices to parents in exercising their democratic responsibilities.

* The law gives parents certain specific rights to choice, information and consultation about their children's schooling. (See the SCC's *The Law of the School*, for further details.)

And now, with the setting up of school boards, a new dimension is brought to bear in children's schooling. Parents are given special rights to participate in school matters by electing fellow parents onto school boards to represent their interests. School boards also strengthen the role of parents not just in regard to the education of their own children but also to the education of children in general at the school.

Parents as partners
The idea of parents working in co-operation with school staff to secure the satisfactory education of their children has now gained widespread professional acceptance. In her book *Parents as Partners,* one educational writer, Gillian Pugh, has defined partnership as:
"... a working relationship that is characterised by a shared sense of

purpose, mutual respect and the willingness to negotiate. This implies a sharing of information, responsibility, skills, decision making and accountability."

This kind of partnership can be and has been put into practice in various ways, with some of the most successful initiatives, for example, involving parents and teachers in home-school learning projects in reading.

This booklet suggests how school boards can help to promote this relationship between parents and teachers with reference to:

*   the school's arrangements for consulting parents
    about their children's education (Section 3);

*   the school's provision of written information for parents (Section 4);

*   the school's policies and practices that are of parental interest or
    concern (Section 5).

As John Bastiani has written in his book *Working with Parents:*

"..... ultimately it is individual schools and teachers who must be the most important focus in any attempt to improve home-school relations."

However, he goes on to say:

"It is, however, far too complex a task for schools to tackle alone. In the end, success in this area needs the combined efforts of the education service as a whole, with its wider perspectives and command of additional material and human resources, its potential for providing knowledge and practical support, drawn from the advisory and support services."

It is in the spirit of these principles that this booklet has been written.

3: Bringing home and school together

The law gives school boards considerable freedom to decide how to carry out their legal duty to promote contact between home and school. Apart from having a specific duty to promote the formation of PA/PTAs, school boards are not expected to adopt any particular approaches to home-school contact. They can promote contact through meetings, the written word, or both. They can work directly with parents and school staff to promote contact, or indirectly through the school's PA/PTA. In working out their approach to this task, school boards will want to take into account such factors as the size of the school, whether the school is a primary, a secondary or a special school, and the existing level of contact between parents and staff.

School boards can perhaps, however, best get started on their task in the following ways:

* School boards can appoint a committee or working party to develop school policy on home-school links and to put forward practical suggestions. Since up to half of the committee members need not be on the school board other parents and school staff could be involved.

* School boards can familiarise themselves with what has already been written about home-school relations in their training materials and in some of the publications listed at the end of this booklet. *Working with Parents* by John Bastiani and *Involving Parents* by Alastair Macbeth are especially recommended.

* School boards can set aside time to discuss various approaches to the development of home-school links with a view to identifying good practices.

* School boards can monitor and review the school's existing policies and practices in this area with a view to recommending possible changes. Reviews could include surveys, consultations and interviews with parents and staff.

Where appropriate the school board could urge the headteacher to adopt as official school policy any practices it might advocate, albeit within a framework of parent-teacher partnership. This is most likely to be achieved through a process of *mutual support* between parent and teacher members of the board on the one hand, and *close consultation* between the board and the headteacher, on the other. The school board could recommend that a statement of new or existing school policy on developing links with parents should appear in the school's handbook for parents, and possibly in a separate school board booklet as well if resources allow. (Methods of funding school board publications are discussed in section 4.) In the rest of this section, we suggest a number of ways of bringing home and school into contact.

Creating a parent-friendly school

Impressions of a school may be formed by parents as soon as they step through the school door. Visible and other signs may affect how welcome or at ease parents feel there. Parents with negative feelings about their own schooldays will want reassurances that their child's school is a friendly place to be in. School boards could consider ways in which the school might be made increasingly welcoming to parents, for example, through:

*   signs and notices clearly marked at school entrances or doorways offering words of welcome to parents and helping them to find their way round the school;

*   appropriate briefings for staff, teaching and non-teaching, about receiving parents at the school and dealing with letters and telephone calls from parents;

*   a visitor's book, inviting parents to write down their impressions of the school.

Depending on accommodation available, the school board could suggest the provision of a visitors' room for receiving parents.

Parent-teacher consultations

Consultations between parents and teachers can be divided into *private consultations* about an individual child and *group consultations* concerning children in a class, year or school group as a whole. Consultations also imply a process of *two-way* communication between parents and teachers, in recognition of the educational partnership between parents and staff.

The law gives school boards the opportunity to make their views known to the headteacher about the school's arrangements for parents and staff to consult one another (sub-section 12(3) of the School Boards (Scotland) Act 1988). The headteacher must first of all provide the school board with information about these arrangements, verbally or in writing, or

both. The board may make "representations" on these arrangements to the headteacher. The headteacher must then consider these representations and reply to them, although he or she need not act on them. School boards are free to comment on any aspect of these arrangements, for example, the nature, timing and conduct of consultations. These and other aspects of parent-teacher consultations are now considered in detail.

Private consultations

Private consultations between parents and teachers about an individual child possibly constitute the most important form of home-school liaison. Their main purpose is to allow parents and teachers to plan jointly for the next stage in the child's education, building on information about the child's past performance and, as far as possible, the child's own preferences concerning future provision. If they are to be genuinely two-way, private consultations will involve:

* parents discussing with teachers their child's development and pursuits at home and the teacher discussing with parents the child's progress and well-being in class;

* parents and teachers drawing one another's attention to what they see as the child's main strengths and main weaknesses or difficulties;

* parents expressing their own wishes or preferences concerning future provision for their child, including provision of any specialist support that the child may require;

* teachers advising parents how they can provide support and encouragement at home.

Where it is not existing practice, the school board could suggest to the headteacher that written guidance might be issued to parents and staff in preparing for private consultations with one another, taking into account the above sorts of considerations. This guidance could appear in the school's handbook for parents and/or be attached to the children's school report.

Similarly, the school board could also suggest the provision of two-way reports, which some schools have now successfully introduced. In such a document, parents as well as teachers make their own written observations about their child's progress and development and use this as a basis for consultations in planning future provision. Two-way reports serve as an important reminder that parents as well as their child's teachers bear a primary responsibility for their child's education. To encourage and help parents to fill in the two-way report, parents could be asked specifically for their observations on the teachers' written remarks in the report, on their hopes or concerns about their child's progress, on the development and well-being of their child at home, and on any other matters they would like to draw to the school's attention.

School boards at secondary schools will also want to consider with the school, in the light of school practice, to what extent private consultations should include participation of the child as he or she gets older and what arrangements should be made for private consultations with pupils staying on at school after reaching the age of 16 or for adult learners returning to school. At schools where individual teachers of different secondary school subjects may see hundreds of pupils in a week, school boards will need to give some thought to the length and frequency of private consultations.

School boards will want to take into very careful account arrangements for consulting parents of children with special educational needs, whether recorded or unrecorded. Many of these children will be attending mainstream as well as special schools and private consultations between their parents and teachers could be of critical importance in planning for their next stage of schooling. For more information, see the SCC's *In Special Need: a handbook for parents of children and young people in Scotland with special educational needs*.

Group consultations

Parents and teachers can also consult one another:

* at class level to discuss work being done by pupils in class, especially in primary school and the lower levels of secondary school;

* at year-group level to consider such matters as starting, transferring or leaving school, choice of courses, examinations, careers, etc.

* at a school level to discuss matters of general interest or concern, such as school policy on discipline, playground safety and supervision, curricular issues, and school spending.

Class consultations   Consultations between parents and teachers of pupils in a particular class or teaching group have become established practice in schools in other European countries, such as Denmark, Italy and Sweden, but are a relatively new idea in Britain. In a report of the

European Parents' Association, *Training of Parents as Class Delegates*,
Alastair Macbeth has written:

> "Class level liaison is especially relevant since the class is the basic
> administrative and educational unit of the school and all parents
> with children in one class share the same educational experience
> through their children; meetings at that level can be informal,
> friendly and welcoming; the class provides a small enough `cell' for
> there to be one or two class delegates who can contact the other
> families personally to get them involved, so that the chances of
> overcoming the well-known parental reluctance to attend are
> improved; and finally, the teacher can collaborate with a class group
> of parents with considerable economy of time."

Class consultations thus provide an ideal opportunity:

* for parents to get to know each other and their child's teacher(s) in a
  much more intimate way than larger, more formal meetings;

* for encouraging parents to take an active, detailed and informed
  interest in their child's schoolwork and possibly become involved in
  particular projects;

* for briefing parents on how they can reinforce what is learned
  in class through support and encouragement at home;

* for helping parents to convey to teachers their own views,
  preferences and concerns about their children's education;

* for teachers to draw upon parents' knowledge of pupils and
  parenting skills in the planning and development of future work in
  class.

Parents who are perhaps less confident in dealings with teachers at a
one-to-one level or who are put off by large gatherings of parents are
likely to find class consultations the most congenial way of becoming
involved in their child's schooling. Compared with larger gatherings of
parents and staff, they have the special advantage of reflecting the
interests and concerns of all parents attending them. Class meetings do,
of course, involve careful planning on the part of staff, ideally backed by
teacher training, but they offer a lot more scope than other sorts of
meeting for working with parents at an informal level.

Class consultations could also function as a mechanism for maintaining contact between the school board and the body of parents as a whole. Each school board member could be assigned responsibility for maintaining contact with particular class or year groups. Each class or year group could, in turn, appoint a parent to liaise with the school board. Consideration could also be given to the idea of class or year groups appointing their own delegates to sit on class councils, as in French schools, to consider classroom matters at a more formal level: interested readers should refer to chapter 6 ("Class-level liaison") of Alastair Macbeth's book *Involving Parents* for a detailed account.

Year-group consultations   In smaller schools, meetings of parents from a year group of pupils are likely to share the purposes and advantages of class meetings (and at some schools will of course be identical to class meetings). But even at larger schools, year-group meetings are likely to have an important function in bringing together parents who can closely identify themselves with one another's concerns or problems as their children reach a particular stage of schooling.

Year-group consultations are of particular value to parents of children who are starting school for the first time or who are transferring to secondary school. Staff can explain to parents the approaches to teaching and learning at these stages of education. Parents can be invited to discuss curricular and other aspects of the next stage of their children's schooling and be encouraged to voice their anxieties or concerns.

Year-group consultations are also relevant for parents of pupils making a choice of course or preparing for public examinations. Parents can be informed about the choices available, the school's policy on presenting candidates for examinations, and arrangements for consulting them and their children individually. Parents can be encouraged to comment on these provisions and again to voice any concerns or difficulties.

The timing of these consultations would obviously be a crucial factor and should include provision for follow-up consultations at classroom or private levels.

Whole-school consultations   There are occasions when it is appropriate to call meetings of parents of all pupils to consider matters of general interest or concern, notably curricular matters (including curricular changes), but also other concerns such as discipline, school spending, and staffing. Such consultations provide an important forum for parent-professional dialogue about key policy issues and help to ensure that schools are responsive to parental concerns and are accountable for their actions. This aspect is dealt with at greater length in section 5 of this booklet.

Meetings can be enlivened and involve parents more by being broken up part of the time into smaller discussion or working groups. Parents who are cowed by large audiences may "come to life" in a small group. Enough time should be left for questions and discussion from the floor, which may mean keeping speeches short. Parents and staff should have an opportunity to socialise at the end of the meeting. Meetings could be linked up with a school social, concert or other event to encourage attendance!

In the light of its findings about current school arrangements, the school board could draw up its own checklist of suggestions for boosting parent participation at meetings.

Consultations: other considerations

Whatever the nature of parent-teacher consultations, school boards may wish to comment on or put forward their own suggestions about the following aspects:

Timing: School boards could comment on or make suggestions concerning the frequency of parent-teacher consultations and the points in the school year at which they should take place. For example, private consultations could take place, say, two or three times a year, possibly after the exchange of written reports. They should normally take place outwith school hours or at times when parents can make themselves available.

Access: School boards will want to give special consideration to arrangements for consultations with parents who cannot visit school, for example, because of work, child care or other commitments, illness or infirmity, transport problems or other difficulties.

Having regard to school resources, contractual arrangements and other circumstances, the board could consider the scope for initiating:

* home visiting schemes: school staff speak to parents in their own homes at agreed times;

* phone-in surgeries: parents speak to their child's teacher by telephone at agreed times, an approach which has operated successfully in Scandinavia for many years;

* special transport in school or community minibuses or through car-share arrangements, with parents perhaps paying a small charge;

*   toddlers' creches, run by parent volunteers.

Suggestions could be put to the headteacher and, if appropriate, representations could be made to the education authority with a view to policies or securing additional resources.

Invitations: School boards could advise on the *general* wording and presentation of written invitations to parents, having regard to such questions as:

*   Do the invitations give parents enough encouragement to attend consultations? Are they friendly enough in tone?

*   Are the nature and purposes of the consultations properly spelt out? Do the invitations remind parents of their educational role?

*   Are parents presented with ideas or issues for possible discussion at the consultations? Could invitations include a checklist of possible questions to put to staff?

*   Do separate invitations need to be issued to parents with limited understanding of English?

*   Do invitations include a reply slip for parents to fill in? Are they issued at sufficient notice for parents to make babysitting or other arrangements?

*   Do invitations inform parents about alternative arrangements for consulting them if they cannot attend at the arranged times?

Participation: School boards may need to give special consideration to ways of involving parents who, aside from any practical difficulties, rarely or reluctantly take up invitations to attend consultations - the parents teachers most want to see but least see. Perhaps these parents are discouraged from attending because of bad memories of their own schooldays; because their child is not doing well at school, or because they are having too many difficulties of their own. Or they may simply feel that there is no need for them to become involved or that they would not be made to feel welcome at the school. Again, having regard to school resources, contractual arrangements and other circumstances, the school board could consider the scope for the initiation of:

*   home-support schemes: support groups or workshops run by "outreach" education staff at community, family or other centres for parents who have difficulties in dealings with the schooling system;

*   school liaison with social work and other agencies in regular contact with parents;

*   community education classes for parents, introducing parents to the working of the schooling system and their role in it, with practical projects to get them involved.

Again suggestions could be put to the headteacher or taken up with the education authority.

Conduct: School boards could comment on the actual arrangements for consulting parents, having regard to the following sorts of questions:

*   Are consultations taking place in an atmosphere in which parents and teachers will feel sufficiently comfortable and relaxed with each other? This is likely to relate to arrangements for receiving parents at the school, choice of venue, seating arrangements etc.

*   Is there provision for ensuring that private consultations really do take place in conditions of privacy - outwith earshot of other parents, free from telephone interruptions or other avoidable distractions?

*   Do the consultations provide parents and teachers with sufficient time for a proper exchange of information and viewpoints? Private consultations lasting for up to 15 minutes would seem reasonable, for example.

*   How do demands on staff time for reporting and consulting relate to other duties? Are the demands made reasonable and such as to aid rather than impede general teaching duties?

Follow-up: School boards could comment on any arrangements by the school for following up consultations with parents. They could recommend, for example, that a record be kept of future action agreed to between parents and teachers at private consultations. A copy of this could be issued to parents, reminding them of their part in any agreed course of action.

Co-ordination: The school board could recommend that a member of staff be remitted to co-ordinate home-school liaison. The person appointed should be a senior member of staff who commands confidence and respect among colleagues and parents. Home-school liaison teachers have functioned with considerable success at schools in several parts of the UK, including some parts of Scotland. The home-school liaison teacher, who would receive a special responsibility payment, would be in overall charge of the planning of consultations between parents and staff, having regard to such considerations as the timing and conduct of meetings in close consultation with those concerned.

Home-school contact: other approaches
Apart from formal consultations parents and teachers are likely to come into contact with each other in various other ways, and school boards will want to consider how they might be promoted:

Parent participation in classroom activities Parents may have much to contribute to children's education through their own presence in the classroom, particularly in the early stages of schooling. Schools are increasingly recognising the importance of parenting skills in teaching children to read, for example. Their presence may be important to children having difficulties settling down at school. Their presence also serves as an important reminder that parents, as well as teachers, are their children's educators.

School boards may wish to comment on school policy or practice on parent participation in classroom activities, perhaps suggesting how this might be developed, though cautioning against the use of participation as a means of getting menial or trivial tasks done.

Extra-curricular activities School clubs, sporting events and other extra-curricular activities provide parents and teachers with important opportunities to meet one another informally or socially. School boards could encourage parents to help with the running of extra-curricular activities or contribute useful skills or experience of their own.

Special visits Parents may from time to time visit (or telephone or write to) the school for advice or information or to bring to the school's attention some problem, concern or complaint. School boards could issue their own written guidance to parents about raising concerns or complaints to do with their children's schooling. School boards could also comment on and recommend changes in procedures normally followed by the school in handling such complaints or concerns.

Promoting new initiatives School boards might consider less standard ways of bringing parents and teachers together, drawing, say, on experience, in other parts of the UK or from abroad (Alastair Macbeth's *The Child Between: a report on school-family relations in the countries of the European Community* is a mine of information in this respect). For example, the Danish parents' organisation Skole og Samfund has invented a board game *Dialogue*, now adapted for use in the UK, which encourages parents and teachers to discuss children's learning in an amusing and non-threatening way (further details on request from the Scottish Parent Teacher Council or the education department of Glasgow University).

4. Keeping parents informed

Promoting good home-school links also means giving parents written information about what the school is doing. A regular flow of written information helps parents to understand the school's policies and practices, for example, in the curriculum, assessment of pupils, homework, discipline, and pastoral care. The information serves as a written reminder that parents, in partnership with school staff, bear responsibility for their child's education. The information is useful to refer to at meetings between parents and school staff and saves school staff having to repeat the same information endlessly to a succession of parents. It could also be important for parents in selecting a school for their child. Moreover, written information offers an account of what the school is meant to be doing and a basis upon which parents can form opinions or raise concerns about stated school policies or practices.

Types of written information for parents

Written information for parents can broadly be divided into:

* information about individual children, as in school reports and school records;

* information about the school or a particular stage of schooling including information about what and how children are taught, as well as on practical matters such as school holidays and transport;

* information issued by the education authority or by central government about various policy or practical matters, for example, on provision for children with special educational needs.

Much of this information is now required by law. For example, parents of pupils must have been issued with written information, usually in a handbook, about the school's educational aims, what is taught there, assessment, arrangements for parents to visit the school, homework, discipline, school meals, school transport, and various other topics. School board members are referred to the SCC's *Keeping Parents Posted* for further details.

In promoting home-school liaison, school boards will have an interest in the content and presentation of much of this information, particularly the school's handbook for parents. We suggest later on in this section what role the school might play here.

School board information for parents

School boards must report to parents at least once a year on their activities (sub-section 12(2), School Boards (Scotland) Act, 1988). School boards are free to decide how to do this. One approach would be for school boards to issue their own written statements, in the form of public reports, for parents. Written reports have the advantages of reaching more parents than reports given orally at meetings, and they provide a permanent record of the board's activities. Depending on costs and other considerations, school board reports could be issued to all parents two or three times a year, through newsletters or bulletins. Alternatively or in addition, the board could issue an annual report, providing a general overview of its work. The board could arrange for reports to be discussed at parents' meetings.

Content of reports

Reports could cover either a range of different topics or focus on just a few topics. The school board, in preparing reports for parents, could draw on the annual and other reports it is entitled to receive from the headteacher. School boards will probably want to relate reports to their functions as laid down in law. These concern:

Home-school links   The board could report on how it has been fulfilling its statutory duty to promote home-school links, preferably coupled with a statement of school policy on home-school liaison.

Parents' or parent-teacher associations (PA/PTAs)   The board could report on how it has been carrying out its statutory duty to encourage the formation of a parents' or parent-teacher association at the school or on the support or co-operation between the board and the existing parents' association. Parents could be reminded from time to time of the differences between the functions of the school board and the PA/PTA.

Representations   The board could mention any responses it has made to statements of school policy on the curriculum, the assessment of pupils, homework, discipline, school uniform or other matters. The replies of the headteacher or the education authority to these representations could also be reported on. If in summary form, reports could refer parents to other documents for detailed information.

Parents' resolutions   School board reports could mention any resolutions passed at meetings of parents convened by the board and say how the board has responded to them.

Books and materials   The board, which is responsible for approving school spending proposals on books, materials and other items, could say how much has been spent per pupil on these items.

Pupils' attainments   In the annual report presented to the board the headteacher must include details of pupils' attainments (but not the attainments of individual pupils). The board may want to consult the headteacher about the appropriate method of presenting this information to parents, given the influence of out-of-school factors, such as home background, on children's learning. The report on attainments may include examination or test results but need not be limited to them; it could cover other achievements by groups of pupils in school, including those which are not formally assessed, such as class projects, drama or musical productions and sporting achievements.

School-community links   The school board is also under a duty to promote links between the school and the community. Reports could mention contacts established between the school and local community groups. They could also mention here what efforts the board has made to promote community use of the school.

Delegated functions   School boards can be delegated with various functions, for example, responsibility for minor school repairs or school meals (See introduction and Appendix 1). Reports could say how these functions have been carried out.

Financial information   School boards must be provided with information about the running costs of the school and capital spending related to the school. The board can also reasonably request other financial information. Reports could contain statements summarising this information and refer parents to other documents for further details. The board could also mention any representations it has made to the education authority about this expenditure and the authority's reply to them.

School board budget   School boards could report on the use of their budgets for administration, training and other running costs.

Other matters   School board reports could draw attention to other matters which do not relate directly to their functions but which are nevertheless of concern, for example, school closures, spending policies and other issues affecting more than one school.

Members of the school board   Reports could remind parents of the

names of members of the school board, indicating whether they are parent, staff or co-opted members and saying how they can be contacted.

Preparation of reports

Preparation   The school board could appoint a committee to prepare reports for parents, giving an opportunity for other parents and staff to become involved (up to half of the committee members need not be members of the school board). The board will also want to involve and closely consult the headteacher as far as possible in the preparation of reports. Reports prepared by a committee would need to be submitted to the board for approval.

Presentation   School boards will want to ensure that their reports to parents are attractive and interesting to read. A checklist of suggestions is given at the end of this section.

Production   The board will have to fund publication costs out of its own budget. To minimise costs, the school board could consider pooling resources with the PA/PTA to produce reports jointly. It could also consider approaching local firms to sponsor production or take out advertising space.

Distribution   Copies could normally be distributed via pupil post and made available at meetings of parents convened by the board. They could also be issued on request to parents contacting the school for copies.

The school handbook

As explained above, parents of pupils at the school will have been issued with a handbook describing the school's arrangements for educating their children and the school's policies and practices on various issues. Although the school board has no basic legal responsibilities or functions relating to the handbook, the board may nonetheless be concerned that it is well written and presented and tells parents what they need to know.

School boards could become involved by offering their own comments or suggestions at the initial preparation or revision stages. For example, the board could comment on the coverage of various topics or the language or style in which the handbook is written. The board will be particularly interested in the handbook's treatment of home-school issues and in promoting through the handbook the idea of parents as partners with staff in their children's schooling. Again, school boards could refer to the checklist of points at the end of this section.

Alternatively, the board could, with the agreement of the education authority, take on delegated responsibility for the preparation of the handbook. Working in close consultation with the headteacher, the board could appoint a committee to draft or revise the handbook. The board would need to check that the content meets the statutory requirements and to take into account any guidelines issued by the education authority.

Points on presentation and production

School boards involved in the production of their own reports, school handbooks or other publications, could carry out the following "quality control" checks:

Language:	Is the text written in a style or tone appropriate to the audience (friendly, informal, non-patronising)?
	Does it adequately convey the need for parents and teachers to co-operate in the education of pupils?
	Is the text too long-winded/concise?
	Will particular words or phrases be understood properly by all parents?
	Should the text be written in more than one language?
	Should a glossary of educational terms commonly in use be included?
Layout:	Is the text attractively laid out (imaginative use of space, headings and sub-headings)?
	Are paragraphs too long?
	Is the right size or sort of typeface used?
Content:	Is there a list of contents/index?
	Are topics arranged in some sort of logical order?
	Is coverage of particular topics too detailed/glossed over?
	Are readers directed to sources of further information?

Illustrations:	Is clear and imaginative use made of drawings, photographs and diagrams?
	Is the cover eye-catching?
Production:	Is the publication securely bound or too flimsy?
	Could use be made of desktop publishing facilities?
	Could parents or other volunteers assist with production work (operating photocopying or other equipment, collating and stapling pages)?

5 Representing parents

So far we have suggested how school boards can promote co-operation between home and school by helping to bring parents and teachers into closer personal contact and by ensuring that parents are properly informed about their children's schooling. School boards can take this a stage further by helping to make parents' points of view on various matters known to school staff, the education authority, and, if appropriate, to central government. School boards are under a legal duty to ascertain as often as they consider necessary the views of parents on matters they are concerned with. They also have special duties to consider any resolutions passed at meetings called by parents to discuss the activities of the board. School boards will also want to take parents' viewpoints into account in commenting on policy statements or reports issued by the headteacher or education authority. Before taking on any additional responsibilities (delegated functions) the board may also want to consult parents. These and other processes indicate that school boards have a very important role in representing parents.

One of the main justifications for school boards is that they offer a channel of communication between parents and the school and give parents a greater say in the running of schools. The more open this communication is, the more likely it is that schools will be responsive to concerns expressed by parents. A responsive school will not necessarily grant the wishes of the school board but it is likely to take careful account of those wishes before reaching any decisions, and it should be willing to explain and justify its course of action.

Scope

School boards have considerable scope for putting parents' viewpoints forward on a whole range of issues, for example, school policies on or arrangements for:

curriculum and assessment of pupils, including provisions for consulting parents (and pupils) about curricular or course choices/transfers

provision of homework

presenting candidates for examinations

safety and supervision of pupils

discipline and school rules

guidance and support for pupils

school book spending

school holidays and opening hours

They may also need to consult parents on issues affecting more than one school, such as proposed changes in school catchment areas or school intakes, school closures and school transport.

Key tasks for the school board, especially parent members, are:

* giving parents adequate opportunities to make their views known on particular matters;

* ascertaining exactly what parents' views are;

* dealing with divergent or conflicting viewpoints;

* presenting parents' viewpoints to school staff, the education authority, central government, etc;

* reporting back or responding to parents.

Role of school board members

In his book *School Boards: from purpose to practice*, Alastair Macbeth has distinguished between school board members functioning as 'trustees', at one extreme, and as 'delegates', at the other:

"It is left to the personal judgment of trustees to represent their group or wider communal well-being as they consider appropriate since they cannot reflect all the individual views of their constituents. They have no obligation to refer back, between elections, to those who elected them. A delegate, on the other hand, will feel obliged not only to report back to those who elected him, but on major issues to seek their guidance or even their authority to act, procedures which can be cumbersome and slow."

He expresses preferences for neither of these extremes but suggests that it is appropriate to see school board members as occupying a position somewhere in between: in practical terms this involves school board members

"..... keeping in constant contact with those who elected them, especially any interest groups, seeking views when uncertain (if necessary through referenda) and being aware of current concerns, but when in a board meeting still having the right to decide individually."

The main tasks of school boards in this area, then, are:

*   encouraging and motivating parents to make their views known, especially through the PA/PTA (if one exists), but also through individual contact with parents, school board reports and so on;

*   actively seeking out or canvassing parental opinion, again through the PA/PTA and possibly also through surveys and home visits;

*   liaising with the PA/PTA at the school in taking joint initiatives;

*   making special efforts to ascertain the views of parents who would otherwise have difficulty in making their viewpoint known, for example, because of language or cultural barriers, difficult home circumstances, and physical disability. Once more, the PA/PTA may be the most valuable means through which this work is done.

Dealing with representations

Having drawn together parental viewpoints, the school board then has the task of working out how to handle them. A lot will depend on the complexity or sensitivity of the issue concerned. A relatively straightforward issue, such as whether the school should have more computers, will require different handling from a sensitive issue such as school discipline. The board will probably want to draw up a written record or summary of parents' points of view, highlighting any divergent or conflicting viewpoints. It will also need to assess how representative these viewpoints are of the parent body as a whole. It may want to hear the views of the headteacher and other staff before preparing any reports or submissions. Finally, the board may want to make arrangements for informing parents of the outcome of consultations, for example, through report-back meetings or newsletters.

School boards and PA/PTAs

The PA/PTA is an important forum for canvassing parental opinion on various matters as well as for promoting parental involvement in school generally. An active PA/PTA and an active school board should go hand in hand: the two bodies should be seen as complementing, not competing with, one another.

The PA/PTA has a role in:

* developing a distinct parental viewpoint on educational and other issues of home-school concern;

* encouraging parents to meet to discuss matters with which the school board is concerned;

* helping to make parents more aware of the functions and activities of the school board;

* providing practical assistance to the school board in arranging parents' meetings, publishing newsletters, undertaking surveys, etc;

* possibly assisting with and perhaps providing candidates for school board elections.

School boards have a legal duty to promote the formation of PA/PTAs. This could include helping a group of parents to get a PA/PTA started, and drawing on the practical advice and information provided by the Scottish Parent Teacher Council (see list of addresses and further reading at the end).

The school board could provide continuing support to the PA/PTA by:

* inviting PA/PTA representatives to attend school board meetings, including committee meetings;

* arranging for parent members to be present at PA/PTA meetings (a parent member of the school board could be invited to become an ex officio member of the parents' association committee);

* working jointly with the PA/PTA in certain activities, for example, in commenting on reports or statements of policy issued by the head teacher or education authority;

* consulting PA/PTA committee members in planning meetings, issuing reports, and so on.

The Scottish Parent Teacher Council's booklet *The Active PTA* contains suggestions for a wide range of parents' association activities which the school board might want to encourage or support.

School boards and parents' groups at classroom level

As suggested in the previous chapter, school boards may have a role to play in promoting the formation of parents' groups to act as channels of communication between the school board and the body of parents on issues of concern at specific stages of education.

School boards and other parents' groups

School boards may also want to establish links with local parents' federations, parents' action groups campaigning on various issues, and national bodies such as the Scottish Parent Teacher Council. While school boards need not commit themselves to agreeing with the policies or views of these organisations, they are likely to benefit greatly from an exchange of ideas and information with them. They may also want to establish links with other voluntary organisations in the area with an interest in children's schooling, such as groups for under-fives, single parents, ethnic minorities, handicapped people, and so on.

Local federations of school boards

Occasions are likely to arise where school boards wish to come into contact with one another to exchange ideas and information and perhaps present a joint view to the education authority or central government on various issues. One approach is for school boards to form their own federations, at a district, education division or regional council level. In some areas of Scotland, there are already federations of PA/PTAs, which could be usefully mirrored by school board federations. Alternatively, school boards belonging to a secondary school and its associated primary schools could hold combined meetings to discuss matters of common interest.

National confederation of school boards

Local federations of school boards could also form the basis of a national association or confederation of school boards.* Many national organisations represent different sectors of the education profession - headteachers, teachers, administrators - but the Scottish Parent Teacher Council, which currently represents about 520 member PA/PTAs, is at present the only national body in Scotland giving voice to parents' interests and concerns. A national organisation representing school boards would therefore be of great value. Alternatively, a national association of parent members of school boards might be formed to

---

* Shortly before this booklet went to press, an initiative to form such an organisation was already under way.

pursue matters of purely parental concern. In most western European countries parents have their own national organisation to reflect parent rather than parent-teacher interests; Scotland has no such national body, although the SPTC has been quite successful in reflecting the parental dimension at national level. School boards could debate the advantages and disadvantages of different types of grouping. A national organisation could have a special role in:

*   making representations to government ministers and lobbying MPs on matters of parent-teacher concern;

*   promoting new training initiatives for school board members, for example, training in representational work;

*   keeping member school boards regularly informed of national and other developments which have a bearing on their work.

6. School boards and home-school contact: the way forward

This booklet has provided school boards with a range of ideas to help them carry out their legal duty to promote contact between parents and school. Emphasis has been given to the importance of parents and teachers working together as partners in the educational process, given the influence of support from the home on achievement in school. We have suggested how school boards can promote home-school partnership by monitoring and advising on the school's arrangements for parents and teachers to consult one another on educational matters, by helping to keep parents informed about schooling matters through written communications, and by taking into account the viewpoints of parents on issues of current educational concern.

School boards will need the support of both parents and professionals in carrying out these and other tasks. Parents will need to be reminded of their responsibility, in co-operation with school staff, for the education of their children, with the PA/PTA playing a supportive role in this respect. In turn, staff will need to be prepared to work co-operatively with the board as far as their sense of professionalism and available resources (staff time and money) will allow.

In promoting home-school contact, school boards in all probability will have to take on a *proactive* role: initiating their own ideas and activities for developing home-school contact, for which this booklet is simply a starting point. As a first step, school boards could review the ideas and approaches we have suggested, confer with parents and staff at the school, and then draw up their own plans for promoting home-school contact.

School boards should if necessary consider pressing at local or national level for any additional resources needed to put home-school partnership initiatives into practice. With the right level of professional commitment and good management of school resources, some initiatives can be achieved at no or little extra cost. Others, however, may call for additional staffing, particularly initiatives for reaching out to parents in disadvantaged communities with little or no involvement in children's schooling. The availability of additional resources for such initiatives is to a great extent a function of the commitment of those in government (local and central) to home-school partnership. School boards can play a key role by explaining to government why home-school partnership is so important in helping children to take proper advantage of their schooling.

Appendix 1

SCHOOL BOARDS AND THE LAW

School boards are bodies of parents, school staff and "co-opted" members involved in the running of the school. They have a special duty to promote good relationships between the school and parents, and they have a number of other basic functions laid down in law. They can also be given additional, "delegated" functions. They replace school councils, which were abolished at the end of October 1989. Each school (other than a nursery school) is entitled to have its own school board, financed by the education authority, but schools which are so small that there are not enough parents to serve on the board as members may be allowed, under certain circumstances, to run without one. The size of each school board varies according to the size of the school (number of pupils on the school roll at a certain date).

As with other parts of this guide, this section should not be regarded as the 'last word' on the law to do with school boards - this rests with the courts. The examples of how the law is expected to work in practice are intended as illustrations not as statements of the law.

Home-school communication

School boards have certain duties to promote parental involvement in school education.

* The board must encourage home-school contact, school links with the local community, and the formation of parents' associations and parent-teacher associations (PA/PTA). The school does not have to set up a PA/PTA if parents do not want one, but, short of a court ruling on the matter, parents probably cannot be prevented from setting one up at the school. The board may also want to have formal links with the PA/PTA, through representation on any of its committees or through other meetings and communications, although the board is not legally required to give PAs/PTAs formal recognition.

* The board must find out as often as it thinks necessary what parents' views are on matters they are dealing with. It may, for example, want to consult parents about school book spending, curricular matters, school discipline, policy on homework and so on. This could be done through meetings of parents arranged by the board or

through letters or questionnaires sent to parents inviting their views. Parents are also free to make their views or concerns known to the board or to individual members of the board without waiting for the board to initiate the process. (see also *parents' meetings* below.)

* The board must report back to parents of pupils at least once a year on its activities. The board can do this through meetings with parents, through written reports, or both.

* The board must consider any resolutions relating to its activities passed by meetings of parents arranged by the board. School boards are also obliged to consult and report back to parents on any delegated functions they might have, for example, to do with school repairs and maintenance, school meals, how pupils' progress is reported to parents and so on.

The headteacher must provide the board with information about the school's arrangements for parents and teachers to meet or consult one another. The headteacher must also consider and reply to any points of view from the board about these arrangements. The board might want to suggest, for example, how meetings should be run, either with parents individually or with groups of parents. The headteacher need not, however, act upon this advice.

Parents' meetings

If requested by enough parents, the board must arrange meetings of parents to discuss its activities or draw up related resolutions. The request for a meeting must come from at least 30 parents of pupils or from a quarter of those entitled to vote at the last election of parent members of the board, whichever is less. Parents must say in writing why they want the meeting and what matters they wish to raise or which resolution they want to propose.

The board must post to parents, in good time, the date, place and purpose of the meeting saying what matters are to be raised or resolutions proposed. It must arrange for one of its own members to chair the meeting and for other members to attend (whatever number the board considers necessary). Any members of the board, the headteacher, and parents of pupils may attend and speak at the meeting, as may anyone else invited by the board, such as teaching or other education authority staff. The chairman decides on the procedure at the meeting and may rule out discussion of any matter or resolution not mentioned in the request for the meeting. Only parents of pupils at the school may vote on resolutions. The law does not say how the resolution should be passed - it could be by a show of hands or by secret ballot, for example. The board must consider any resolution passed at the meeting, although it need not act upon the resolution.

Information and reports

The education authority must provide the board with any information it may reasonably request from time to time about the school it represents or about the authority's provision of education: for example, information about school staffing, advisory services, or provisions for pupils with special educational needs. The authority is unlikely to respond to requests for information it considers unreasonable, such as confidential information about pupils or staff.

The headteacher must provide the board, as soon as it has been set up, with statements of the school's policies on the curriculum, the assessment of pupils, discipline, school rules and the wearing of uniform. The headteacher must also advise the board of any changes in these policies, although he or she need not do so until those changes have actually taken place. To prevent possible misunderstanding the headteacher will probably want to put policy statements in writing but does not have to.

The headteacher must also issue an annual report to the board, including a report on the level of attainment of pupils in the school (but not on the attainments of individual pupils). The board and headteacher are free to consult one another about what the annual report should cover. The headteacher must also provide any other reports or information the board may reasonably require. Reports might, for example, cover such matters as the repair and maintenance of the school, playground safety and supervision of pupils, school meals, school staffing, extra-curricular activities and so on. The school board may put its point of view to the authority or headteacher about any of this information. The authority or headteacher must consider these views and reply to them, but need neither seek out nor act upon the views of the board.

Advice to boards

The headteacher has the right, and, if requested by the board, the duty to give advice to the board on any matter it is concerned with. The education authority must also do so if requested by the board. The board must consider any advice given, although it need not necessarily act upon that advice.

The headteacher is also entitled, but not required, to attend meetings of the board. Other members of school staff could be invited to attend and speak at meetings, with or without the headteacher being present. The director of education, nominated officials of the education authority, and regional or islands councillors for the electoral division of the school can also speak at and attend meetings. They are not members of the board and the board may listen to but is not bound to accept any advice they may give. There is nothing to stop councillors from becoming members of school boards in other electoral divisions if they qualify as parent, staff or co-opted members.

The board can invite to its meetings anyone it wishes to receive advice from, for example, people with specialist knowledge of the curriculum, representatives from voluntary organisations, or members of national bodies concerned with education.

Staff co-operation

The education authority must take whatever steps are appropriate to ensure that the headteacher and staff at the school are "available when necessary" to allow the headteacher to fulfil his or her school board duties and to carry out any competent decisions of the board. This means that school staff, in doing work connected with the board, cannot be required to do more than is possible under their terms and conditions of employment.

Books and materials

The education authority must provide the headteacher each year with money for school books and other teaching materials ('capitation allowance'). It must also provide money for "other purposes" it thinks fit, such as money for field trips. The school board is responsible for approving proposals the headteacher must draw up on how this money should be spent. (If there is no school board, the headteacher is free to spend the money as he or she thinks fit.) If the proposals are not approved by the board the headteacher will have to submit new or modified proposals.

Certain safeguards must be observed by the headteacher in drawing up proposals and by the board in approving them. The school board and the headteacher must have regard to any guidance given by the education authority. They must also take account of any of the authority's policies on the school curriculum and ensure that the authority's legal obligations are met, for example, the authority's duty to secure "adequate and efficient" school education. Failure of the board to observe these requirements could lead to the education authority or the Secretary of State taking legal action to enforce them. This might happen, for example, if the board has failed to approve spending proposals after a

reasonable period of time has passed. The education authority, school board and headteacher may, if they wish, consult one another before the capitation allowance is fixed or the spending proposals on school books and materials are drawn up. The board could complain to the authority if it thinks that the amount is not enough.

Financial information

The education authority must provide the school board with statements on the school's running costs (e.g. on salaries, repairs and maintenance) and capital expenditure (e.g. on improvement work and new buildings). The School Boards (Financial Information) (Scotland) Regulations 1990 set out what financial information should be presented. The authority must consider and reply to any comments the board may make about this information. The authority must also provide the board with any other financial information it may reasonably request. This could cover, for example, expenditure for other schools in the area.

Financial powers

The school board can raise funds (except by borrowing), spend the money raised, and receive gifts, so long as this is for the school's benefit and the headteacher is consulted. The board must keep proper accounts of its expenditure. The board can invest money but cannot own or acquire land and buildings. It may want to appoint its own treasurer. The board cannot levy fees or charges for school education provided by the education authority, although the authority may delegate to the board the power to fix charges for school lettings or other matters.

The education authority must provide the board with funds to cover administrative expenses, training and other expenditure. Extra funds must be provided to cover the costs of any additional responsibilities delegated to the board by the authority. The authority decides how much money the board gets for these items, but the board must be consulted beforehand. The authority must make the money available as and when the board requires it.

Should the board cease to exist, any property owned by the board is passed on to the education authority, but the authority must use it for the benefit of the school. Should the board be re-established, the property goes back to the board.

Use of school premises

The school board is responsible for controlling the use of school premises outwith school hours. It has a duty to encourage the "community" use of school premises. This could include use of the school by voluntary organisations, for example. The board must, however, follow any directions given by the education authority, which continues to fix charges for the use of the school, except when this power has already been delegated to the board. The board must also take account of any use of school premises or equipment for further education. The education authority, the college council concerned and the person in charge of the body providing further education must be consulted by the board about any changes affecting further education at the school.

Occasional holidays

School boards, after consulting the education authority, can fix occasional holidays during school term time. There are legal limits to the number of days schools may be closed for holidays.

Delegated functions

School boards can be given additional responsibilities, known as delegated functions. These might include taking charge of the repair and maintenance of school buildings, enforcement of school attendance, administration of staff salaries or other school expenditure, determination of school policy on discipline and so on. These functions can be delegated to the board at its own request, or they can be delegated at the initiative of the education authority, but only if the board agrees.

Functions can be delegated for a limited or for an indefinite amount of time. The board may, for example, want to work with delegated functions for a trial period before deciding whether to take them on permanently. The board can also hand back its delegated functions, provided that certain procedures are followed. The authority can lay down conditions under which the delegated functions must be carried out, for example, a condition requiring the board to seek the authority's approval of spending above a certain amount. The board may consult parents before deciding whether to request or agree to a delegated function, but it is not legally required to do so. Extra money must be given to the board to carry out delegated functions.

Certain functions may not be delegated:

*   The board can not take formal responsibility for employing or dismissing school staff, including non-teaching staff (but the board, short of employing or dismissing staff, can be given power to select staff, other than senior staff, with the education authority, as employer, confirming the board's choice).

* The board can not formally select headteachers, depute and assistant headteachers (the board is already involved in selecting these members of staff through representation on appointments committees, as described below).
* The board can not control the curriculum or the assessment of pupils (but the way in which results of assessments are reported to parents can be delegated).
* The board can not close down the school, move the school to another site, or merge the school with another one.
* The board can not end or set up special classes or a stage of education at the school, such as nursery or sixth year classes.
* The board can not decide on policies for admitting pupils to the school (but school boards can be given responsibility for the actual organisation of school admissions).

If the school board asks for additional responsibilities, the education authority must let the board know within six months whether or not it has agreed to the request, with reasons for any refusal. If the authority agrees to the board's request, it must issue a draft "delegation order" to discuss with the board and reach agreement on. If agreement is not reached after two months and if the board so requests, the current draft order must be referred to the Secretary of State for a final decision.

Before reaching a decision, the Secretary of State must consider the views of the board and the authority, both of whom can be required to provide the Secretary of State with additional information or documents. Unless satisfied that the additional responsibilities of the board would interfere with the good running of the school, the Secretary of State must direct the authority to grant the delegation order. The Secretary of State may attach conditions to the order, saying how these additional responsibilities must be carried out.

If the authority refuses a request from the board for additional responsibilities, the board may call a ballot of parents on the issue (see below for more details about ballots). The ballot paper must say what the school board's proposals are and what the authority's reasons for refusing the delegation order were, together with any reply to the authority by the board. If more than half of the parents vote in favour of the proposals, the authority can decide again whether or not to delegate the function. If the authority still refuses to do so, the board may refer the matter to the Secretary of State for a decision. The Secretary of State then follows the same rules as above.

If the education authority initiates the process, a draft of the order must

be sent to the school board for its consideration. If the board does not agree, the additional responsibilities cannot be delegated to the board.

Under certain circumstances, the authority can suspend, end ('revoke') or modify a delegation order. Certain procedures must be observed by the authority before this can be done. If necessary, the matter can be referred to the Secretary of State, who again must follow rules similar to those described above in deciding whether the order should be revoked, suspended or modified.

Relations between the school board and the education authority

School boards must carry out their functions so as to ensure that the education authority is not prevented from fulfilling its legal obligations. These obligations include, for example, securing adequate and efficient school education, observing equal opportunities, and securing health and safety and other legislation. This would prevent the school board, for example, from obstructing or unduly delaying spending on school books and other educational materials. A complaint could be made to the Secretary of State or a case brought to the Court of Session against a school board which fails to carry out such a legal obligation (see under "Complaints" and "Legal Action" in *The Law of the School*).

The school board must respond to any reasonable request the education authority may make for information about its activities. For example, the authority could ask the board for information about its efforts to promote home-school relations or community use of school buildings.

School boards are regarded as acting as agents of the education authority in their dealings with third parties, such as tradesmen and transport operators. This means that contractors can claim from the authority any loss, damage or injury arising from proven negligence of the board. Claims cannot be made against individual members of the board so long as they were acting in good faith.

Membership of school boards

School boards consist of parent members, staff members and co-opted members.

Parent members are parents of pupils at the school elected by other parents of pupils there.

Staff members are teachers or instructors at the school, whether full- or part-time, elected by other such staff at the school. Teachers or instructors attached to more than one school can sit on more than one school board.

Co-opted members are neither parents of pupils at the school nor teachers or instructors there; they are chosen by the elected members of the board.

People entitled to serve as staff members on the board cannot serve as parent members on that board; but they may be entitled to serve on the boards of other schools at which they have children. People entitled to serve as parent or staff members cannot serve as co-opted members.

Regulations lay down the size of the school board:

School roll	Parent members	Staff members	Co-opted members
1-500 pupils	4	1	2
501-1000 pupils	5	2	2
1001-1500 pupils	6	2	3
Over 1500 pupils	7	3	3

At single teacher schools, with a headteacher only, school boards have no staff member, three parent members and two co-opted members. (Since visiting teachers can also stand as staff members, only a few schools, in practice, may be single teacher schools.) Any changes in pupil numbers above or below the above limits (on 31 August before the next two-yearly election of parent members) must be followed by adjustments to the size of the school board.

Term of office.   Board members hold office for four years, except that at the end of the board's first two years, half the parent members must stand down (or the largest number less than half if the board has an odd number of parent members). Those standing down must be selected by drawing lots if parent members otherwise fail to agree on who should stand down. Parents of children who have been at the school longest or are due to leave earliest may agree to stand down, for example.
A board member, if still eligible to serve, may hold office for more than one four-year term if re-elected (or re-appointed as a co-opted member). Members may resign at any time. The board may remove members who are unable to carry on with their duties because of physical or mental illness or incapacity. They can also be removed for failure to attend three consecutive meetings provided that the board has met over a continuous period of at least six months.

By-elections.   These must take place as soon as practicable after the initial election to fill any remaining vacancies for parent members. By-elections must also be held within three months if parent or staff members leave the board and their term of office has still more than six months to run. Members who are no longer qualified to stand in a future election, for example, as a result of their child leaving school, can remain members of the board if their term of office still has less than two years to run.

Co-opted members.   Once established, the board must appoint the required number of co-opted members "as soon as practicable". Co-opted members need not be appointed immediately; they need only be appointed after the board has had reasonable time in which to consider whom to co-opt. At denominational schools, at least one of the co-opted members must have been nominated by the church or denomination concerned. Young persons (aged 16 to 18), including senior pupils at the school, may also be co-opted. School boards can choose the sorts of people they co-opt, but they are expected to co-opt people who can usefully add to the experience or expertise of people already on the board. Co-opted members could include parents of former pupils who are no longer eligible to serve as parent members. They could also include members of school staff who are not teachers or instructors, such as school secretaries.

School board members can claim from the education authority travel and subsistence allowances for attendance at board meetings or carrying out other activities approved by the authority, for example, attendance at appointment committees. They are entitled to release from employment to attend school board meetings but they have no automatic right of loss of earnings allowances although they can claim allowances for attendance at appointment committees. In practice, the school board is likely to meet at times that suit its members.

Elections

Education authorities are responsible for organising school board elections. Elections are held every two years for half* of parent members on the board and every four years for staff members. By-elections must also be held within three months of any casual vacancies arising, except when the term of office has less than six months to run. The authority must appoint a returning officer and draw up an election scheme in accordance with government guidance; different arrangements may be made for different schools. After the first elections, the authority can

---

* Or the largest number less than half if the board has an odd number of parent members.

delegate the actual organisation of the election, although not drawing up the election scheme itself, to the school board. Copies of the election scheme should be issued to the school board and available for the public to see.

Election timetables.   The election scheme should give the latest dates for eligibility to vote, to nominate candidates, to stand as a candidate in an election or ballot, to submit election statements, and for the issue and return of ballot papers, the counting of votes and announcement of results.

Electoral rolls.   The election scheme should refer to arrangements for keeping accurate and up to date electoral rolls of parents and staff eligible to vote at each school, including arrangements for resolving disputes about eligibility to be on the electoral roll. Authorities are expected to take reasonable care that all parents of pupils are given a chance to get their names put on the electoral roll. Authorities might do this, for example, through notices sent home via pupils or announcements in the local press. Both parents are entitled to be on the electoral roll, including step-parents and parents living apart from their children. So as many as three or four parents per child may be on the roll. Parents of children at nursery classes attached to a primary school are also entitled to be on the school's roll. The electoral roll cannot be made public, but individuals are entitled to check that their own entry on the roll is correct. The roll can only be used for school board elections and ballots.

Voting.   Each parent has one vote, regardless of how many children he or she has at a particular school. Parents with children at more than one school can vote in more than one election or ballot, however. Each voter can vote for as many candidates as there are vacancies at the election. For example, if there are vacancies for three parent members, each parent can vote for up to three candidates. Voters cannot give more than one vote for one candidate. Members of school staff who have children at that school are also entitled to vote in elections for parent members, but they cannot stand as candidates for election as parent members. Elections must be by secret ballot and parents must be given the chance to vote by post.

Organisation of elections and ballots.

Each scheme should include details of arrangements for: -

-      ensuring secrecy of ballots and preventing people voting more than once (it must also mention the circumstances in which voting papers are considered spoilt)

- recounts of votes
- deciding on the results of the election when two or more candidates get equal numbers of votes, for example by lot
- recording and notifying the results of elections and ballots
- preserving voting and other relevant papers for at least six months after the election or ballot.

* **Nominations.**   Nomination forms may be sent with the election notice, which should otherwise say where forms can be obtained, for example, at school. Parents or staff wishing to stand as election candidates must sign the form, together with the signatures of any proposers and seconders, who must be eligible voters. Parent nominations normally require a proposer and a seconder, and staff nominations a proposer only. Election schemes can relax these requirements for nominations at small schools, say, a proposer only at parent elections. Self-nomination of staff members is allowed at schools with fewer than four members of staff entitled to vote.

* **Election statements.**   In elections of parent members, candidates may submit an election statement of up to 250 words. Candidates could say, for example, why they are standing and what contribution they hope to make to the work of the board. This statement is circulated with the ballot papers. The education authority could refuse to circulate statements which incite racial disharmony, contain obscenities or make the authority, as publishers of the statement, criminally liable in some other way. The authority is also expected to avoid circulation of statements which are defamatory, referring them back to candidates and pointing out to candidates their possible liability at civil law.

* **Uncontested elections.**   If the number of candidates equals the number of vacancies, candidates are automatically declared elected and no ballot takes place. If there are fewer parent candidates than vacancies for parent members, candidates are declared elected, and a by-election to fill the remaining vacancies must be held as soon as practicable. If there are still vacancies for parent members after that, the board must be disbanded ("disestablished"), but it may be re-established whenever enough parents make a written request to the education authority in writing. The request must come from at least as many parents as there are places for parent members on the board. A fresh election must then be held; the original candidates, if still eligible, may stand again. A fresh election to fill vacant places must in any case take place between 22 and 24 months after the last election, followed, again, if necessary, by a by-election. A board with vacancies for staff members may still be set up or continue to run.

* **Ballot papers.**   In elections, ballot papers are sent to parents on the school's electoral roll; these could be sent to them by "pupil post" or mailed to parents directly. They will give the names of candidates, and should be accompanied by any election statements. Parents must be given time to return their ballot papers by post. Arrangements must be made to ensure secrecy of the ballot when votes are counted. Replacement ballot papers can be issued to cover unintentional loss or damage.

In ballots to find out whether a majority of parents are in favour of the board having certain additional functions, the ballot paper should be accompanied by a statement from the board saying what additional functions are sought and why. There should also be a statement from the education authority saying why it has refused the board's request for additional functions, together with any reply to the authority's reasons by the board.

* **Count of votes.**   The count should be open to inspection by candidates and, in the case of ballots of parents, by members of the school board and representatives of the education authority. Places on the board go to candidates with most votes; no minimum percentage vote is necessary for any candidate to be elected. Winning candidates may be selected by lot in the event of a tie. The education authority is responsible for making the results known locally, for example, through the local press or school newsletters, although parents or staff need not be informed individually. Ballot papers must be kept for at least six months after the election or ballot of parents in case results are challenged.

* **Post-election procedures.** The education authority may keep a register of school board members, which should be updated as new members join or others leave, together with a record of their length of office. The authority arranges the initial meeting of the board and subsequent elections and by-elections (except when the board has been given responsibility for organising elections).

School board meetings

School boards are responsible for drawing up their own rules ('standing orders') about how their meetings should be run. To save each board having to devise its own, however, model standing orders could be drawn up by education authorities for school boards to adopt or adapt. These rules stay in force unless altered or suspended by the board. At least one third of the board's full membership must be present ('in quorum') before the board can meet. A seven-member board, for

example, would need three members present to be 'in quorum'.

The board decides how often it should meet. That is likely to depend on the size or other circumstances of each board. The board might meet once every month or six weeks, for example. Meetings are likely to take place in school, but they may take place elsewhere, for example, at local community centres. The board draws up its own agenda and can discuss any item to do with the school or education generally.

* **Chairing of meetings.** The board elects its own chairman and vice-chairman from the parent and co-opted members (i.e. staff members cannot chair meetings). The board could appoint a temporary chairman until co-opted members have been appointed.

* **Voting.** The chairman (or in his or her absence, the vice-chairman) has a second or 'casting' vote if an equal number of 'yes' and 'no' votes have been cast. Casting votes may not be used to appoint co-opted members office bearers or committee members. In such cases, decisions are reached by drawing lots.

* **Minutes.** Records ('minutes') must be kept of what is discussed and decided at school board meetings. The minutes must have been signed by the person chairing the meeting at which the minutes have been agreed. Copies must be sent to the education authority if requested. They must also be available at the school for anybody to see.

* **Committees.** School boards can set up their own committees to consider particular matters. Such committees might, for example, deal with home-school liaison, curricular matters, school finance, and so on. Up to a half of the committee members need not be school board members. The school board can decide how committees should be run, including setting their 'quorum'. Committees must consider and report back on matters referred to them by the board; they are not allowed to reach decisions binding on the school board.

The school board is required to appoint a clerk to arrange meetings, take minutes, circulate papers to board members, and undertake other clerical work (the exact duties of the clerk are not laid down in law). The clerk, unless already a member of the board, may be paid for this work out of the board's budget. Clerical duties could be undertaken by the school secretary, for example.

Public access to school board meetings and documents

Members of the public (including the press) are entitled to attend school board meetings and to see agendas, minutes and reports connected with meetings. However, the public can be denied access to documents or admission to meetings or parts of meetings dealing with certain confidential matters, namely items relating to:

* school staff, former staff or staff appointments.

* individual pupils, former pupils or prospective pupils.

* any information which the board is legally obliged not to disclose, for example, information which the board is under a contractual obligation to hold in confidence.

* any other matter which the board thinks should be handled on a confidential basis because of its nature (the board need not give reasons for withholding access, but it would do well to show that it was justified in doing so).

Appointment of senior staff

The school board must be represented on the committee set up by the education authority to appoint senior school staff: headteachers, depute headteachers and assistant headteachers. The committee conducts any interviews of candidates for the post and recommends who should be appointed; the education authority must normally accept the committee's recommendations, which could include a recommendation to re-advertise. Equal numbers of school board and education authority nominees must sit on the committee. The school board need not nominate only its own members - it could nominate somebody not on the board but who has a specialist knowledge of or concern with the appointment. The authority need not nominate its own members or officials either, although in most cases it is likely to do so.

For the headteacher appointments the committee must be chaired by one of the authority's nominees - and for the other appointments, the committee must be chaired by headteacher of the school. Staff members of the school board or co-opted members who are pupils at the school may not sit on the appointments committee. If there is no school board for the school, the committee consists of the authority's nominees only and, for non-headteacher appointments, the headteacher of the school, who chairs the committee.

Appointment committee procedures are governed by the rules applying to sub-committees of the education authority. The authority cannot control the activities of the committee, however. At least three eligible candidates must normally be on the short list for the committee to

consider. The authority can re-advertise if there are fewer than four eligible applicants; if there are still fewer than four applicants after re-advertising, or if the authority decides not to re-advertise, then the total number of applicants forms the short list.

For headteacher appointments, the authority must draw up a short list of candidates, which must first be submitted to the school board concerned before it is considered by the appointment committee. The board must meet without its staff and any co-opted pupil members to consider applications. The board can add names to or remove names from the list, so long as any additions are from the list of eligible applicants. The board cannot reduce the list to fewer than three names. If there are fewer than four names on the original list, the board cannot alter it, but the board can submit comments which have to be considered by the appointment committee. These comments may be about each candidate or general comments, such as a request for the post to be re-advertised.

These procedures do not have to be followed for other appointments. The authority submits the short list directly to the appointment committee.

The director of education or his or her nominee is entitled to attend and advise the appointment committee, which must consider this advice, that is, concerning the professional suitability of each candidate. The authority must appoint one of the candidates unless the person recommended by the committee should turn out after further enquiries not to be eligible for the post, when the whole procedure must start off all over again. (In practice, this should rarely happen, as the authority will have carried out its own checks before short listing candidates.)

Combined schools

When two or more schools combine (whether remaining on the same sites or not), the existing school boards are formed into an "interim" school board until the school board for the combined school is ready to take over. One of the main tasks of the interim school board will be to assist in the selection of a new headteacher for the school. Delegated functions cannot be given to interim school boards.

Schools without a school board

A school may be without a school board either because it is too small to have one or because the board has not been set up or has been disbanded (as a result of not having the required number of parent members - see under *uncontested elections* above).

In the first case, the education authority need not take steps to set up a school board if, because of the small number of pupils at the school, there are not enough parents to serve on the board. The authority may only do so, however, with the agreement of the Secretary of State. It must nonetheless take the necessary steps to set up a school board if this request is made, in writing, by at least as many parents as would be required to serve on the board. The authority must also reconsider its decision not to set up a board if it thinks that there has been a significant increase in the number of pupils at the school; it may also reconsider its decision at any other time. In either instance, the authority must then arrange for school board elections to be held, following the rules already described above.

At schools which are too small to have a board, the education authority or the headteacher must provide parents of pupils with information that would otherwise be provided for the board. This includes information relating to school policy on the curriculum, the assessment of pupils, on discipline, school rules and the wearing of school uniform, and on the school's arrangements for consulting parents. It also includes an annual report on levels of pupils' achievements and other aspects of the school's work and a statement of the school's capital and running costs. The authority or the headteacher must take account of and reply to any views parents give in response to such information or reports. Such information and reports need not, however, be provided to parents at schools where the board not been set up or has been disbanded, although the authority could agree to make it available.

School boards and self-governing schools

With the support of a voting majority of parents and the agreement of the Secretary of State, a school can become self-governing. The school takes over complete responsibility for its running, outwith education authority control, with funding of the school coming from central government. School boards play an important role in the procedures which must be followed before a school can become self-governing. For further details, see **How to Become a Self-Governing School: guidance for school boards.**

Where to find out more:

School Boards (Scotland) Act 1988

School Boards (Scotland) Regulations 1989 (SI 1989/273)

Education (Publication and Consultation Etc)
(Scotland) Amendment Regulations 1989 (SI 1989/7739)

School Boards (Financial Information) (Scotland) Regulations 1990. (SI 1990/1277)

Scottish Education Department, "School Board Elections and Ballots," *Circular 3/89* and "School Boards: financial information", *circular* 12/90 (obtainable from the Scottish Office Education Department, New St Andrew's House, Edinburgh EH1 3SY)

Scottish Education Department, *School Boards: a guide to the legislation* (obtained from Publications Section, Scottish Office Library, Room 144, New St. Andrew's House, Edinburgh, EH1 3SY.

The Times Scottish Education Supplement, *School Boards Guide*, 1989 (obtainable from TSES, 37 George Street, Edinburgh EH2 2HN).

Alastair Macbeth, *School Boards: from purpose to practice,* Scottish Academic Press, 1990.

Alastair Macbeth, *Involving Parents*, Heinemann Educational Books, 1989.

Self Governing Schools Etc. (Scotland) Act 1989.

Scottish Office, *How to Become a Self-Governing School: guidance for school boards* and Scottish Office Education Department, "Self Governing Schools: statutory provisions", Circular 14/89 (both publications obtainable from Room 4/11, The Scottish Office Education Department, New St Andrew's House, Edinburgh EH1 3SY).

Crown copyright 1990
First published 1990
Revised 1991

Appendix 2

List of recommended reading

The following publications, presented in alphabetical order by author, are mostly obtainable through bookshops, libraries, or the organisations listed in Appendix 3. Those which pay special attention to Scotland are marked with an asterisk (*).

Advisory Centre for Education, **Planning your school prospectus, ACE.**

A practical step-by-step guide to preparing a school handbook or prospectus for parents, with emphasis on making the handbook attractive and interesting for parents to read.

John Bastiani, **Working with Parents: a whole school approach**, NFER-Nelson, 1989.

An indispensable source of ideas and practical guidance on the development of home-school relations. The book explains how to plan a 'whole school' programme on links with parents, who are seen as an important 'educational resource'. Subsequent chapters give practical guidance on written communication and face-to-face contact with parents, working with parents in classrooms, class meetings, curriculum evenings, home-school agreements and annual reports to parents. The book provides practical application of ideas discussed in two earlier books by John Bastiani in the series, **Parents and Teachers 1: Perspectives on Home-School Relations**, and **Parents and Teachers 2: From Policy to Practice**.

European Parents' Association, **Parents and School Management in Europe, EPA,1990.**

A good descriptive outline of the structure, functions and membership of school management bodies in most of the countries of the European Community, including details of the "class council" system in Italy, the "discipline council" in France, and the "school conference" in Germany. Other EPA publications include:

Training of Parents as Class Delegates, Written School Reports for Parents in Europe, Parental Choice of School in Europe, Homework in Europe, Safety and Health in Schools, Parents' Associations and Teachers' Unions in Europe.

*Alastair Macbeth, **The Child Between: a report on school-family**

relations in the Countries of the European Community, Commission of the European Communities, Education Series No.13, 1984.

Detailed and wide ranging account of home-school practices in EC countries at the levels of the individual child, the parents' group, and the school.

*Alastair Macbeth, **School boards: from purpose to practice,** Scottish Academic Press, 1990.

Essential reading for school board members wishing to understand more about their participative and representational roles and the purposes and functioning of school boards. The author points out that although school boards have a number of subsidiary aims, such as promoting contact between the school and the community, "the main thrust of the legislation is to provide a forum in which those with different but overlapping duties for the education of children can consider common interests through representatives".

*Alastair Macbeth, **Involving Parents: effective parent-teacher relations**, Heinemann Educational, 1989.

An excellent introduction to the practice of home-school relations, which emphasises the role of parents as co-educators and explains why parental involvement in school is so important. A minimum 12-point programme of home-school practice is proposed, involving a "signed understanding" between parents and staff. Other chapters suggest how home-school communication and support for disadvantaged families can be improved, how PTA/PAs can be developed, how the class can be a focus of home-school liaison, and how a `whole school' approach to liaison can be fostered by school boards and governing bodies.

John MacBeath, David Mearns and Maureen Smith, **Home from School**, Jordanhill College, 1988, and J. MacBeath **Home from School - its current relevance**, Jordanhill College, 1989.

School board members will find much of relevance in this major report and its sequel, based on research among parents and teachers, which concludes that schools could do much more towards communicating effectively with parents. Among the main recommendations for improving home-school links are better management of parent-teacher meetings, home-visiting schemes, and proper grievance procedures for handling complaints by parents.

National Consumer Council, **The Missing Links between Home and School**, 1986.

Uses survey findings and the results of group discussions to recommend improvements in home-school communication, involving a strategy which goes beyond simply producing school brochures and parents' evenings. For example, schools are urged to review their arrangements for handling parents' complaints and for receiving early notification of problems.

Gillian Pugh, **Parents as Partners**, National Children's Bureau, 1981.

Describes ten different schemes for giving parents support through groupwork and home visiting schemes and training them to become educators of their own children.

*Scottish Consumer Council, **The Law of the School: a parents' guide to education law in Scotland**, HMSO Books, 1987.

Detailed legal guidance is given on 56 educational topics arranged alphabetically and supported with cross references and sources of further information. Topics covered include admission and attendance of pupils, books and materials, choice of school, clothing and uniform, curriculum, discipline, exams and assessment, exclusion from school, guidance, homework, school closure, sex discrimination, and transport. The volume comes with a special supplementary guide to the School Boards (Scotland) Act. Essential reading for school board members wanting to understand the law on schooling matters.

*Scottish Consumer Council, **Keeping Parents Posted: information about children's schooling and other educational matters**, HMSO Books, 1988.

Signposts parents to sources of official and other information about children's schooling, for example, in school reports and records, school handbooks, council papers, and inspectors' reports. Guidance is given about how to read these documents, and shows, through examples, how to put the information to good use. Address and reading lists.

*Scottish Consumer Council, **In Special Need: a handbook for parents of children and young people in Scotland with special educational needs**, HMSO Books, 1989.

This handbook explains to parents the very important role they can play with professional staff in the assessment and recording of children and young people with special educational needs. It describes the recording process in detail and the range of support children may require. It then raises some of the wider issues affecting provision which parents or their representatives (on PTA/PAs, school boards) may want to take up with the education authority or central government. Annotated reading and address lists.

*Scottish Education Department, **Talking about Schools: surveys of parents' views on school education in Scotland**. Series titles: **Main Findings; What Makes a Good School?; Relationships between Home and School; Teachers and Headteachers; Learning and Teaching,** HMSO, 1989 and 1990.

This series of booklets provides a wealth of information on the opinions of parents on a wide range of issues connected with their children's schooling based on in-depth interviews and questionnaire data. The booklet on relations between home and school, for example, reports on parents' views on and satisfaction with parents' meetings, school handbooks, reports on pupils and PTA/PAs, and letters home. Essential reading for school boards in developing or influencing home-school liaison work.

*Scottish Parent Teacher Council, **Why have a PTA? Setting Up a PTA, The Active PTA** and other publications, which school board members will find indispensable in carrying out their legal duties to promote parent-teacher and parents' associations. The SPTC also regularly publishes information bulletins and submissions to government on various home-school issues. It has issued its own video on parent-teacher partnership, *Back to School - parents in education.*

*Strathclyde Regional Council, **Partnership in Education: a public report**, SRC 1988.

This report on the Partnership in Education Project in Strathclyde describes and evaluates strategies for the development of confidence and skills which professionals and parents need in order to work together. The report concludes that the "diffuse strategy" adopted by the project had been effective in increasing parent-professional involvement, although it will take several years before the impact of the project on children's school performance can be assessed. List of project documents and videos.

Bernard Van Leer Foundation, **Partnership in Education** project reports. Current titles, based on work with parents in schools, include "Parental Involvement: basic ideas to launch your pre-entrant programme", "Workshops for Parents of P1 children", "Postman Pat - a parental involvement programme for library and school" and "Partnership in Education - helping children and adults think, learn and grow together". Reports and publications list obtainable from the Foundation, PO Box 82334, 2508 The Hague, The Netherlands.

Welsh Consumer Council, **Dear Parent: a guide for parents with children starting school**, WCC 1988.

Schools interested in issuing their own introductory guides for parents of children starting school will find this booklet worth referring to. The booklet, written in question and answer format, deals with such topics as parental support at home, choice of school, school meals and transport, special educational needs and parents' meetings.

Magazines and newspapers

Articles on or of interest to school boards frequently appear in the following journals:

Ace Bulletin (six issues a year), Advisory Centre for Education, 18 Victoria Park Square, London E2 9PB

Regularly reports on education issues and developments from a parental perspective and provides a digest of recent publications, including Scottish ones.

School Governor (six issues a year), 73 All Saints Road, Birmingham B14 7LN

Although aimed at members of school governing bodies in England and Wales, each issue contains some features likely to be of general interest to school board members.

Scottish Child (six issues a year), Scottish Child Publications, 40 Shandwick Place, Edinburgh EH2 4RT

Comment, features, and review articles on a wide range of issues affecting the education, health, housing, welfare, etc., of children and young people in Scotland.

The Times Scottish Education Supplement (weekly), 37 George Street, Edinburgh EH2 2HN

News, features, comment and readers' letters on all aspects of Scottish education, plus reports on developments in the UK and overseas. See also the education pages of *The Guardian* (Tuesday), *The Scotsman* (Wednesday), *The Independent* (Thursday), and *The Glasgow Herald* (Thursday).

Scottish Educational Review (twice yearly), Department of Education, University of Glasgow, Glasgow G12 8QQ.

Articles, reports and reviews on research, policy issues and developments in Scottish education.

Appendix 3

USEFUL ADDRESSES

Organisations are listed in alphabetical order (for a more comprehensive list of organisations, see the SCC's *The Law of the School, Keeping Parents Posted* and *In Special Need*).

Advisory Centre for Education
18 Victoria Park Square
London E2 9PB

Provides advice and information for parents, parents groups, and parent governors on a wide range of educational matters. Publishes a bi-monthly Ace bulletin, which includes a digest of current publications.

Association of Directors of Education in Scotland
Education Offices
40 Torphichen Street
Edinburgh
EH3 8JJ

Association of Head Teachers (Scotland)
64 Biggar Road
Symington
Lanarkshire
ML2 6LQ

Commissioner for Local Administration in Scotland
(Local Ombudsman)
5 Shandwick Place
Edinburgh
EH2 4RG

Receives and if necessary investigates complaints relating to the administration of local authority services. Results of investigations are made public.

Convention of Scottish Local Authorities
Roseberry House
9 Haymarket Terrace
Edinburgh EH12

Promotes and represents the interests of local authorities in Scotland through research, reports and seminars.

Educational Institute of Scotland
46 Moray Place
Edinburgh
EH3 6BW

Promotes and represents the interests of teachers in Scotland.

Educational Publishers' Council
19 Bedford Square
London WC1

Promotes and represents the interests of publishers of school books and publishes occasional reports on school book spending.

European Parents' Association
c/o B E J C E
2-3 Place du Luxemburg
B-1040 Brussels
Belgium

Acts as a forum and information exchange for parents' organisations in EC countries and regularly publishes booklets and a newsletter on matters of home-school interest.

Headteachers' Association of Scotland
Park Cottage
21 Victoria Place
Airdrie
ML6 9BU

Professional Association of Teachers
22 Rutland Street
Edinburgh
EH1 2AN

Promotes and represents the interests of teachers in Scotland.

School Boards Support Unit
The Scottish Office Education Department
New St Andrew's House
St James Centre
Edinburgh
EH1 3SY

The unit provides advice and information on request to school boards about any aspect of their work and produces a regular newsletter, *School Boards News*.

Scottish Child and Family Alliance
55 Albany Street
Edinburgh
EH1 3QY

Promotes welfare of children and their families by developing links between professional and voluntary workers, running conferences and training courses, and through publications, including a regular newsletter.

Scottish Child Law Centre
1 Melrose Street
(off Queen's Crescent)
Glasgow
G4 9BJ

Offers advice to children, parents and professionals on law relating to children up to the age of 18; provides a free telephone advice-line; publishes a newsletter, leaflets and booklets; runs conferences and seminars; offers training courses.

Scottish Community Education Council
West Coates House
90 Haymarket Terrace
Edinburgh
EH12 5LQ

Develops and supports community education in Scotland.

Scottish Consultative Council on the Curriculum
(publications)
Gardyne Road
Dundee
DD5 1NY

The SCCC advises the government on Scottish curriculum matters and regularly issues reports and newsletters on curriculum developments.

Scottish Council for Voluntary Organisations
18-19 Claremont Crescent
Edinburgh
EH7 4QD

Supports the formation and development of voluntary organisations in Scotland through conferences, training, information and representational work.

The Scottish Office Education Department
New St Andrews House
Edinburgh
EH1 2SX
(for publications:
Room 323, 43 Jeffrey Street
Edinburgh
EJ 1DN)

Scottish Educational Research Association
15 St John Street
Edinburgh
EH8 8JR

Promotes and reports on educational research in Scotland through seminars, conferences, and publications, including a quarterly newsletter.

Scottish Parent Teacher Council
30 Rutland Square
Edinburgh
EH1 2BW

With well over 500 member parent-teacher and parents' associations, the SPTC represents and promotes the interests of parents on a wide range of educational issues in dealings with central and local government. Annual conference, seminars, information updates, booklets for parents.

Scottish Secondary Teachers Association
15 Dundas Street
Edinburgh
EH3 6QG

Promotes and represents the interests of teachers in Scotland.

The Scottish Office
Information Directorate
New St Andrews House
Edinburgh
EH1 3TD

Issues leaflets and other publications of parent-school interest.

Printed in Scotland for HMSO by (61484)
Dd 287456 C40 8/91